T. S. Poetry Press
New York
tspoetry.com

ISBN 978-1-943120-59-8

Juvenile Poetry / Science
    Rainbow Crow: Poems in and Out of Form [the beautiful science series]
    Author, Megan Willome
    Illustrator, Hasani Browne

Dip into poetry and science with this collection of free verse and form poems.

You'll meet the catalog poem, the rondelet, the clerihew, the senryu, the diamante,

the ghazal, and more— all while learning fun facts about crows.

Companion materials available at tweetspeakpoetry.com/literacyextras

Rainbow Crow

poems in and out of form

by megan willome

illustrated by hasani browne

ts ♥ *literacy starts with love*

Rainbow Crow

Lucky
if you find an albino crow
Luckier
if you find a caramel crow
Luckiest
if you find a rainbow crow
      but only the Lenape know where he'll show.

{ a catalog poem }

Resumé

Convoke in ancient trees.
Ride pigs for kicks.
Opine while looping on the breeze.
War with straws and sticks.
Slide down snowy banks. Never say please.

{ an acrostic poem }

Definitions

An *unkindness* is a gathering of ravens
A *murder* is a gathering of crows
If at night, you feel rather *craven*
Stay in bed and cover your toes.

{ a quatrain poem }

Raven 'n' Crow

Are you interchangeable?
Your essence rearrangeable?
Your danger just as dangerable?

Raven flows. Crow flaps.
Crows caw. Ravens croak.
Raven taller. Crow smaller.

Both black. Both thrive
near humankind, both now
and evermore.

{ a catalog poem }

Natural Selection (a Pueblo Parable)

Two eggs
    One white, one turquoise
Two eggs
    Careful how you tread
One, a parrot, speaking with joy
One, a crow, your peace to destroy
    Choose wisely now
Two eggs

{ a rondelet poem }

Tools

Crows dig with sticks
form hooks from wire
carry water in cups
    but they'd rather carry fire

{ a quatrain poem }

Noah's Crow

Some say a raven scouted land,
proceeding from old Noah's hand.
The raven flew both far and near
but never did return. Oh, dear.

Then Noah sent a soft white dove
who picked an olive branch with love.
When Noah sent her out again
she stayed to rest. The flood did end.

But if instead he'd sent a crow
to look for land, both high and low,
that crafty bird, so sly and wily,
would have returned with poison ivy.

{ a rhyming couplets poem }

Ginger

A crow well-known as Corbie
Landed on a sleeping blondie
I hear he dotes on hair that's red—
I'd better put a hat upon my head!

{ a clerihew poem }

Elementary

We crows, we all attend crow school
and follow different crow-style rules.

Take field trips to the parking lots
and dare the cars to take our spots.

In music class we sing off-key,
our voices cawing lustily.

During math we count our stash
and show each trinket with panache.

We preen ourselves and call it art,
parading before the mini-mart.

And for our test, we have to swipe
a treasure fine, metallic and bright.

{ a rhyming couplets poem }

Blinded

Foolish trusting boy
Left his glasses out for me
Now I see as he

{ a senryu poem }

Lovebirds

Male
proud, flirtatious
bowing, knocking, tail-spreading
King. Queen.
head-fluffing, fanning, gurgling,
supercilious, vain
Female

{ a diamante poem }

Q&A with Crow

Q: How many nests do you have?
A: One for my fledglings
One for my stash
One for my refuge
One for my cash
One for my mistress
One for my mate
One for the pizza I stole from your plate
Q: That was *you?*
A: Gulp!

{ a catalog poem }

Dear Rascal

In August, crows transgress. Poor dog.
Use doggie chow for a round of chess. Poor dog.

They imitate the neighbor, the neighbor's pet.
Who's next? It's anybody's guess. Poor dog.

They heckle the wrens, harass squirrels from a nest,
hector small children. But I digress. Poor dog.

The gods send us crows as a form of address—
don't judge. Your puppy chow could be next. Poor dog.

Dear Rascal. Leave the crows alone. It's for the best.
From your fruitless corvid hunt, rest. Poor dog.

Go chase a chicken instead!

{ a ghazal+ poem }

Old Ms. June

Old Ms. June, she lived alone.
She watched the birdies from her home.
She fed them all with tasty treats.
She cooled their birdbath in the heat.
Until one day she saw a crow.
He came to stay. He would not go.

So Old Ms. June, she got her broom
and chased that bird from night till noon.
But then she found the perfect plan
to drive that bird far from her land.

She opened up her cookbook wide
and loudly read the meals inside:
"Crow Casserole!" and "Crock Pot Crow!"
"Summer Crow Kabobs!" and "Crow Creole!"

On hearing that, the crow skipped town
And never, never came back around.

{ a rhyming couplets poem }

Ventriloquist

Crows throw their voices on the wind
That meow of your cat is really from them
A bark, a cluck, a hoot, a caw
All proceed from their corvid jaw!

{ a rhyming couplets poem }

Double-Cross

Squirrel hides nuts
Unaware he is watched
Crow dives
Knocks squirrel out of tree—

Instantly a crow partner swooshes in
Takes his booty!

{ a free verse poem }

Goodnight Crow

On the thirteenth floor
there was a great green tree
and a big deep nest
and a picture of
a crow swooping past the shore
and there were three little squirrels hiding their pearls
and a diamond ring and a child's blue marble
and mama crow quietly whispering "garble"
Goodnight floor
Goodnight shore
Goodnight crow swooping past the shore
Goodnight puzzle
Goodnight muzzle
Goodnight spoon
And goodnight rune
Goodnight halo
(if you say so)   →

{ a catalog poem }

Goodnight bolts
And goodnight toggles
Goodnight universe
Goodnight marble
And goodnight to the mama crow
        whispering "garble"
Goodnight midnight
Goodnight wind
Goodnight corvids.
Ever wend.

Author's Notes: Crow Encounters

One sunny spring afternoon, a crow stole my son's brand-new glasses. That encounter led to much research, starting with *In the Company of Crows and Ravens* by Dr. John M. Marzluff, a professor of wildlife science at the University of Washington. From that book I learned that a small pair of shiny metal glasses are exactly the kind of treasure that will entice a crow. The more I read about crows, the more I wrote about them.

I should have picked a nicer muse.

Although they steal, torment weaker creatures, and brag with loud caws about their misdeeds, they are not evil. For me, they symbolize life's unwelcome intrusions that transform us. What better place to delve into the many ways and means of crows than with a poetry book — some of the poems are written in form and some in flying free verse. May they change you too.

—M. D. W.

Form & Free Verse

Poetry can be written in form or in free verse. Think of form as a fence—it has boundaries that show the writer and reader where to go. Free verse is *free range*—no fences, no rules. Ironically, free verse can be much harder to write well. A fence can provide structured space for creativity to root and bloom.

The poems in *Rainbow Crow* are a mixture of form and free verse. When I encounter a form that is new to me, like the ghazal (which is ancient), my first instinct is to try writing a crow poem in that particular fenced area. In the case of "Dear Rascal," I added an extra line at the end, just for fun. Sometimes you need to cut a hole in the fence.

Although free verse doesn't have to rhyme, many of the free verse poems in *Rainbow Crow* do. There is something about crows that makes me want to run to the nearest rhyming dictionary. But "Double-Cross" does not rhyme at all, and "Goodnight Crow" is inspired by Margaret Wise Brown's picture book *Goodnight Moon*, a classic that neglected to say goodnight to crows.

Myths, Legends, Stories & Poems

Crows have always interacted with humans. They are in our trash, on our golf courses, and in our business. They have been part of our stories as long as we've had stories to tell.

Tales about ravens and crows can be found in France, Greece, India, Ireland, Jamaica, Scotland, Tibet, and Vietnam, to name a few. They are in *King Arthur*, in Norse legends, and in tales from many native peoples from the Americas, in the lands where the Inuit dwell, and in faraway islands. They are in the works of Geoffrey Chaucer, Charles Dickens, William Shakespeare, Mark Twain, Vincent van Gogh, and modern authors like Max Porter. Poets also have—*ahem*—taken crows and ravens under their wing, including Emily Dickinson, Robert Frost, Mary Oliver, and Edgar Allan Poe.

Notes on the Poems & Their Forms

A catalog poem repeats words or phrases at the beginning and/or ends of the lines.

An acrostic poem uses the first letter of each line to form a word, in this case, *Crows*.

A quatrain poem has four lines that rhyme, in a pattern such as ABAB or ABCB.

A rondelet poem has seven lines, some with eight syllables and some with a four-syllable refrain.

A clerihew poem has four lines, some sort of rhyme, and is meant to be funny.

A rhyming couplet poem has any number of two-line sets that rhyme or close-rhyme.

A senryu poem has three lines and follows the 5-7-5 syllable pattern often found in Japanese haiku, but it is satiric. Kimiko Hahn calls it "haiku's comic cousin."

A diamante poem contrasts opposites in seven lines arranged in a diamond shape.

A ghazal poem is a form of Arabic verse with at least five couplets and a refrain. The last couplet includes a reference to the poet or speaker.

A Little Dictionary

opine	To express an opinion
convoke	To call together for a meeting
craven	(*cray-ven*) Fearful

panache	(*puh-nash*) With style and swagger. The root word means "small wing," like a tall feather atop a helmet
supercilious	(*super-silly-us*) Proud and patronizing. The root word is related to the word "eyebrow," as in *to raise an eyebrow*
heckle	To tease or taunt
hector	To bully
ventriloquist	Someone who speaks in a voice not their own
wend	To follow a wandering road

Poem Notes

Rainbow Crow—White crows and ravens have a condition called albinism. Caramel-colored crows have leucism. While a rainbow crow has not yet been discovered, if you look closely at a crow's black feathers in the sunlight, you will see the iridescent colors of a rainbow. The Lenape (pronounced *leh-nahp-ee*), also called the Leni Lenape, Lenni Lenape and Delaware people, are an indigenous people of the Northeastern Woodlands, who live in the United States and Canada. Some sources claim that their oral literature includes tales about rainbow crows.

Resumé—Crows have been observed doing everything described in this poem, including not saying please.

Definitions—Many animals have words that describe them in a group, such as "herd" or "flock." The unusual collective nouns for crows and ravens describe their character, which can be unkind.

Raven 'n' Crow—Both ravens and crows are corvids, meaning they are in the same bird family with jays and magpies. But ravens and crows have different bodies and behave differently.

Natural Selection—A Pueblo legend tells the story of a person who wished to find a parrot egg, which would bring good fortune when it hatched. A choice had to be made between two eggs, one lovely and turquoise and the other plain and white. They selected the pretty turquoise egg, from which hatched a crow. Whether that was bad fortune or not is up to the reader.

Tools—Crows are renowned for their use of tools. Their brains are similar to those of advanced apes.

Noah's Crow—Stories about corvids are ancient. A raven appears in Genesis, in the Hebrew bible. It's a good thing Noah didn't tangle with a crow!

Ginger—"Corbie" is the Scottish word for crow. They do prefer red-heads and the heads of people who are bald.

Elementary—Crows don't go to school, but if they did, these are the kinds of things they would learn.

Blinded—Small, shiny objects, like bracelets, earrings, screws, and even a child's glasses, may become targets for crows.

Lovebirds—Crow pairs stay together for a long time and flirt with each other anew in spring.

Q&A with Crow—Crows often have multiple nests which they use to hide what they have stolen. They will eat virtually any human food they can get their beak on, including pizza.

Dear Rascal—Ghazal poems are often about longing and asking questions. In this poem the speaker wonders why the dog Rascal is obsessed with crows who are, as usual, up to no good.

Old Ms. June—Cookbooks in the past featured recipes for crow. Old Ms. June would never eat crow, but she doesn't mind tricking one, to protect the vulnerable birds at her feeder.

Ventriloquist—Crows can imitate the voices of other animals and repeat some human phrases, like a parrot.

Double-Cross—Crows may team up to rob a squirrel or other animal of its food.

Goodnight Crow—Based on the rhyme scheme and pattern of Margaret Wise Brown's *Goodnight Moon*, published by Harper & Brothers in 1947.

About the Author

Megan Willome is a writer and editor whose work has appeared in *Magnolia Journal*, *The Fredericksburg Standard*, and the *WACOAN*. She pens the children's book club column at *Tweetspeak Poetry* and is the author of *The Joy of Poetry: How to Keep, Save & Make Your Life With Poems*. Megan lives in Texas and loves crows despite their great mischief— or maybe even because of it.

About the Illustrator

Hasani Browne is a fine artist who was born in the island country of Saint Vincent and the Grenadines. Now living in Brooklyn, she loves to create things as she has imagined them and enjoys inspiring others to do the same. Her favorite bird is a peacock, but after researching and working on this book she gained a new respect for crows because of their intelligence and subtler beauty. The first time she ever saw a crow she was 13 years old and still living island life. The bird, an unusual sighting in that region, was lounging with other species in a plum tree in Hasani's yard. *Rainbow Crow* is her first children's book.

About the Publisher

T. S. Poetry Press is the sponsor of **tweetspeakpoetry.com**, where whimsy and color abounds— around the topics of poetry, writing, and lifelong literacy growth. The Press promotes "poetry for life" and "literacy for life" through free teaching and learning resources, books for grown-ups, and books for children. The publisher is committed to cultivating literacy as one way to create stronger connections between the generations—with themes and co-learning materials that bring together grandparents and grandchildren, parents and children, and teachers and their students.

Additional Resource on Form Poetry

Check out *How to Write a Form Poem: A Guided Tour of 10 Fabulous Forms*, by Tania Runyan—author of *How to Read a Poem: Based on the Billy Collins Poem "Introduction to Poetry."*

www.ingramcontent.com/pod-product-compliance
Lightning Source LLC
LaVergne TN
LVHW072120070426
835511LV00002B/39